WINNING LESSONS

FOR ENTREPRENEURS

IN THE

CONCEPTUAL ECONOMY

WINNING LESSONS

FOR ENTREPRENEURS

IN THE

CONCEPTUAL ECONOMY

JAY MAHARJAN

This book was published by **Venture Loft Publications**

WINNING LESSONS FOR ENTREPRENEURS IN THE CONCEPTUAL
ECONOMY, Copyright © Jay Maharjan

Venture Loft Publications
3960 Howard Hughes Parkway, 5TH Floor
Las Vegas, NV 89169
First Edition: March 2013

Library of Congress Cataloging-in-Publication Data

Maharjan, Jay
Winning Lessons for Entrepreneurs in the Conceptual Economy

ISBN 978-0-9888522-0-4
Library of Congress Control Number 2013935612

Dedication

This book is dedicated to my parents, who believed that I could achieve anything in the world, and to the entrepreneurs out there who have believed in me.

CONTENTS

"As a self-proclaimed entrepreneur, I founded Restaurant.com in the late 1990's. From conceptualizing to fundraising, I know when I'm in the presence of another real life "out of the box" thinker. In-fact, Jay Maharjan has studied under the finest business minds and at a very young age has built a room full of awards and achievements with expansion and continuum."
- Dennis R. Lane, Founder of Restaurant.com

"Change is the law of life. And those who look only to the past or the present are certain to miss the future."
- John F. Kennedy

Preface

We are witnessing the arrival of a new economic model that we have yet to understand fully. Even though this new economic model is unfolding gradually, one thing is for sure: The knowledge economy is changing rapidly.

The knowledge economy came about after management guru Peter Drucker recognized a particular type of workforce in the 1960s and dubbed them "knowledge workers." In the decades that followed, the world saw a sharp increase in productivity, giving knowledge workers a higher level of respect and recognition.

The era of the knowledge economy consistently gave knowledge workers an edge within the general workforce, offering them the kind of job security that was unheard of during the first half of the 20th century. These workers are in for a rude awakening in the upcoming decade. This is also true for small businesses and entrepreneurs, as well as large multinationals that fail to see this change coming.

The knowledge economy gave the United States in particular a tremendous edge in terms of sustaining innovation and creating a healthy job market. The conceptual economy is going to be different. Knowledge workers who adapt to the new norm will weather the storm, but those who fail to change or acquire new skills and understanding will be left behind.

Just as the knowledge economy brought about a fundamental shift in the nature of professions, this new economic model will bring new professionals with strong creative knowledge who will truly understand the need to integrate the "art" aspects of their professions. "Management by Objective" will be taken less literally, and objectives will be created with more foresight and amended on an ongoing basis with new knowledge and information. These objectives will be less stringent and more inclusive based on variables.

The transition will be less glamorous than at the beginning of the knowledge economy, but it will be more methodical and seamless at times. The conceptual economy will see new professionals en masse with enhanced but less disruptive skill sets. Doctors and engineers will still perform their specialized tasks as they did in the knowledge economy, but this time around, they will be challenged to use their right brains more in strategic thinking. MDs of the conceptual generation will be more technologically savvy than most of the technologists in the 20th century, allowing this new breed to bring about changes at the fundamental level of delivering care.

Beyond specialized workers, there will be a whole new set of conceptual workers whose jobs are yet to be created. Most of what has been offered for free so far in the knowledge economy will shift to a paid model.

Conceptual consumers will end up spending less time searching for bargains or free trials, and they will open their wallets for what they believe adds value.

Social media will heavily influence consumers in the conceptual economy, and peer influence will play a key role in consumer buying habits. There will also be a new market for paid, high-end online content, as well as for validated, authenticated news aggregators.

Startup costs for technology companies will come down sharply. Shared resources and communal work efforts like Linux and cloud computing will be a standard way of building infrastructure. There will be a big shift toward coming up with new business models to measure, support, and train conceptual workers.

Analogies for measuring conceptual workers will be similar to the earlier days of the knowledge economy when the companies didn't know how to deal with emerging knowledge workers. At that time, new opportunities emerged for consultants who trained themselves to be experts in consulting to management. (The title later officially became "management consultants," and the likes of McKinsey and Bain & Co. came out of that.) The consulting model thrived in the knowledge economy from big three accounting firms to

ERP consultants to elite management consulting firms that catered to Fortune 500 types.

In the consulting model, there will be a fundamental shift. The future management consultants won't focus on advising companies on processes and methodologies. Rather, they will emphasize human factors and individual human behaviors more often than organizational behaviors. And managing the new generation of technologically savvy, multi-tasking workers with short attention spans will be tough. Management will have to learn ways to train HR departments to recognize and encourage the new norms for this new productive group.

There are many opportunities to be had as entrepreneurs in the conceptual economy and generation. The knowledge economy created an enormous pool of small businesses. In fact, 98 percent of all businesses in the United States are small businesses, and the majority of SMB companies that fall under this category were the brainchild of a knowledge worker. Regardless of the vertical, there is a tremendous opportunity for conceptual entrepreneurs to salvage these companies, sustaining them long enough to transform them into truly conceptual, profitable companies.

Basic business rules and timeless wisdom will still apply, of course. It will be important to ignore glamour. Instead, choose to add value where the majority has ignored it. Address pain points. Be disruptive, but not too much. (Google was and is a rarity.) Learn to defy conventional wisdom and logic. Learn to be a generalist, and ADAPT, ADAPT. Specializing in a dated niche tool is not the way to go!

Most likely, conceptual workers will have to go against the thinking of knowledge workers, who are mostly from the baby boomer generation that tends to hate change. No business school will ever get you ready for dealing with human resources and human emotions.

The conceptual workforce should learn that it is useless to do something very well if it shouldn't be done at all.

Jay Maharjan
Los Angeles, California
February 11, 2013

My Early Corporate America Experience

"The best way to predict the future is to create it."
- Peter Drucker

Holland, Michigan is a beautiful small town on the banks of Lake Michigan. The city is midway between Chicago and Detroit but has a strong personality and culture of its own that was built on its rich Dutch heritage. I got to know it well while I was in college.

In 1996, I was a junior at Pittsburg State University when I got a summer internship position at the Chrysler design center within Johnson Controls Inc. in Holland. I was excited to get this design internship opportunity and, at the same time, take a break from the flatlands of Kansas. I was also excited about the fact that I was one of only two engineering students to be chosen for the cool design internship.

I didn't know what to expect except that I was thrilled to be working for a large corporation and getting paid. I came from a strong educational background, so entrepreneurship was not in my vocabulary (at least not yet). But this was the right path for my career. My family was excited that this internship would lead me to a successful, lasting career at an established multinational corporation, but little did any of us know what was in store for me.

As I drove from Kansas to Holland with David, a Pitt alumnus who had just secured a permanent job at one of Johnson Controls' manufacturing plants, I was hopeful that I might land a job after graduation like David.

I got there on a Sunday. We were housed in a large, reality TV show-style housing complex, and I had three roommates in my apartment. All four of us represented different schools; my roommates were from Notre Dame, University of Michigan, and Michigan State University. I was the only one in the group who was assigned to work at the hip design center. Everybody else in my complex worked at various manufacturing or engineering facilities spread out across the city.

The design center was a state-of-the-art facility with extremely cool automotive design projects going on behind the doors. Artwork hung on the hallway walls, and the corporate culture reflected the rich history of motor town. We saw prototypes from the big three that would never make it to auto expos.

Outside of those walls, however, Holland was an old city with a friendly atmosphere like in the Midwest. It was best known for warm summer days by Lake Michigan, where people from rural Michigan and Illinois flocked for summer activities by the beach. The city was also known for its vast flora and fauna, including its annual tulip festival.

Gary D. was my assigned mentor/boss. It took me the whole summer before I could connect with him on a personal level as a mentor. He was a no-nonsense, extremely bright engineering manager, who surprisingly didn't have a prototypical personality of either an engineer or a corporate manager. His confidence was reassuring to the people who interacted with him.

That summer, I walked into what was turning out to be one of the biggest recall fiascos in the history of the company, and Gary was the project manager for the product that was being recalled.

The issue was with the interior door panels of the 1996 Jeep Grand Cherokee. Because of the wrong adhesives chosen by the engineering team to bond vinyl coverings and the ABS bolster substrate, vinyl covers were peeling off in brand new cars fresh out of the production line. Internal data revealed that roughly ten percent of about 1,400 cars out of the daily production lot were facing this issue.

Gary was under tremendous pressure. His job was on the line, and there was big talk about how to curb this major headache. Chrysler didn't want to stop the line, but Gary didn't have time on his side. Each day that they were unable to come up with a solution spelled another 1,400 cars out of the lot with potential flawed parts. The problem was worse in the hot parts of the country, and the economic implications were enormous. Each time a customer brought back a car for a replacement panel, it cost Chrysler $200-$300 dollars (if my memory serves me).

As I arrived for my first day at work, taking care of me or showing me the ropes was the last thing on Gary's mind. I was already intimidated by the surroundings, and this lack of interest or any sign of warmth to help me fit in didn't help. I was unsure of what I was doing, but it didn't matter. Nobody cared. I was just there as an intern.

The temperature started rising as summer approached. Temperatures crossed the 100 mark in many parts of the country, including Southern Miami, many parts of Texas, and almost the entirety of the Southern California/Nevada region. This was not good news, and it was becoming a nightmare scenario for Chrysler as complaints at dealerships escalated.

Each morning that followed began with an update meeting that reported the fresh tally of complaints. Numbers were being broken down by city, state, and country. It was a nightmare for close to 500 people directly and indirectly involved in the project. The basic math was creeping up on the team. The numbers were staggering: Approximately $260 times the number of voluntary recalls. But the lines were not being shut down. The numbers approached multimillion dollar territory as the complaints rose exponentially.

Even though Gary was at the helm, he was surprisingly calm. He had a quick, dry sense of humor and effortlessly kept the team from going into panic mode. He directed all of his senior engineers to focus on core issues, following a prototypical engineering line of thinking: choosing different materials, adhesives, and manufacturing processes. He directed rigorous validation of new methods. Time was of the essence.

The internal name of the recall was the "ZJ Bolster project," and it wasn't looking good. At the rate it was going, it would take at least a month, if not several months, before manufacturing could effectively make changes in the processes, bringing in new materials. In a worst case scenario, the molds and machines would have to be retooled.

It was a fascinating experience for this young intern as I watched these events unfold. There was the huge pressure of group-think, and there was literally only one solution path for the entire team. As a layperson with a young, naive mind, I started asking, "Why wasn't anybody thinking outside of the box? Why wasn't senior management willing to stop the production when the problems were so blatant? Why wasn't management concerned about handing over keys to cars that were faulty products, potentially deeply affecting the brand?" This could further damage what was already a deteriorating image of brands coming out of Detroit. But, again, who was I to have any say?

One thing I did was start exploring my own solutions to stop the bleeding, while the company only focused on and explored long-term solutions. This was when I guess my innate entrepreneurial drive kicked in. I started tinkering around with cost-effective ways to fix thousands of flawed cars already on the market.

If it cost $260 per recall, there must be a way to bring that cost down, I thought. My immediate question was why dealers were replacing the whole door panels instead of just small defected parts. If we could come up with a way just to replace the specific defected area, we could salvage the rest of the door, saving on parts costs (which I discovered were quite significant). I determined that the cost savings would be in the 90 percent range, which I thought was a remarkable number. I took this information to Gary one late evening and shared my idea.

He appreciated my enthusiasm but politely turned it down, implying that the idea was not feasible and there was more to the overall problem than just replacing the defected areas. He went on to show me in detail that all of the parts on the panel were interconnected and that trying to detach the specific, very imbedded part was not technically pragmatic, especially in the hands of dealerships. They would need to deal with this engineering design issue, and Gary said that dealership staff wouldn't be able to tackle it economically. He added that the quality of work wouldn't be up to par and consistent across different dealerships. So, the clear corporate-wide directive was to keep replacing the entire door panels until the engineering team could come up with a permanent solution that involved choosing the right adhesives and plastic materials.

Gary was convincing in making his points. But I still believed otherwise, even though I didn't let Gary know it at the time. I politely asked him if I could work on my own time weekends and evenings to try to come up with an easy to use mechanical design kit that non-technical people at dealerships could implement. Gary liked my steadfastness and didn't see any harm in letting me think outside the box.

His approval and support also meant that I had access to top engineering and design resources in Detroit. This intern was on a mission! I consulted with personnel in tooling and manufacturing, as well as industrial designers and catalog designers. I came up with an entrepreneurial blueprint, giving myself three weeks to understand the best practices in the industry and how a product is launched within the automotive field. Upon reading various journals, white papers, and industry procedures, I decided not to follow any of them. Looking back at that time now, it's probably safe to say that I was an entrepreneur in the making.

I started testing my prototype using random approaches. Some of my initial ideas didn't include any aspect of engineering. I was a kid with a wandering entrepreneurial mind, very much impressed by the surroundings, just tinkering with stuff.

Nevertheless, through all of that tinkering, I came up with a concept one weekend as to how I, as a layperson at one of the dealerships, could replace the affected area with minimal hands-on technical knowledge.

Then, it was time to get Gary's feedback. Based on his pattern of behavior, I was certain that he would inject his engineering point of view and reject the notion politely.

I caught him in a good mood while he was at a birthday celebration for one of his staff members, and I shared my ridiculously simple idea. To my surprise, he really liked it, and without thinking, he just told me to go for it. This new dose of confidence really helped me. The best part was that he gave his approval for me to go anywhere and meet with anybody at Chrysler, including his superiors, the highest level executives at headquarters in Detroit.

I'm not sure which part I was more excited about— getting this chance to meet with key movers and shakers at the Chrysler corporate channels or getting to be a corporate entrepreneur so that I didn't have a schedule like the other interns. It was also not too bad of a deal that I would get to take the corporate jet between Holland and Detroit on a regular basis to discuss my idea and show my latest prototypes.

This freedom catapulted my desire to make the idea work. I was a 20-year-old intern thinking like a venture-funded CEO in Silicon Valley. The mission was clear. Each day that somebody in the organization did not come up with a solution meant losing another million dollars in dealership maintenance fees.

In the beginning, people didn't know who I was, but I had a clear idea in mind of the people who would be able to help me launch this product and stop the Jeep Cherokee brand from further deteriorating.

Just like in the real entrepreneurial world, I made a lot of friends within the Chrysler culture, as well as people at Ford and GM who frequently socialized with us during non-business hours. We participated in volleyball on the weekends and hastily arranged lunch hour priceless wallyball tournaments. (Basically, it's volleyball played in the confinement of a racquetball court; I know there's a small cult within corporate culture that knows what I'm talking about.) These people taught me many invaluable lessons.

I met my entire roster of contacts for my mini-project out of those groups. I learned early on that the key for an entrepreneur or a corporate worker bee was not to delegate to people but to ask the right questions of the right people. The "art" part of it involved truly making people want to help you. This applies in the real world of entrepreneurship, and it surely also works in the world of corporate entrepreneurship.

A month passed by, and just like a startup entrepreneur, I came up with a basic layout of my prototype. A simple solution involved 16 tinnerman clips, a steel bracket to hold the new product, and a power tool that can be easily found in every household. I also precisely documented the exact amount of time that it would take for the whole process. If the solution was any more complicated or would take more than half an hour for a layperson, the project would never see the light of day.

My next agenda was to sell the idea not only to Gary, but also to his superiors and the whole team from the top down. It was nerve-wracking for me to present freshly updated PowerPoint slides to several groups on a daily basis. At this point, Gary started seeing some potential and began meeting with me every morning to start his day. It really helped. He decided to give me his support in setting up meetings at the highest level at Chrysler Headquarters. Also, he offered me advice that entrepreneurs could relate to: He asked me to go out and visit Chrysler dealers in different parts of the country to see how they would respond to my idea. He was thinking like an entrepreneur and assessing the feasibility of the product.

My trips to dealerships were a series of great learning experiences. It was terrific to receive feedback from the people who would be most impacted by the idea. Knowing your end user is critical whether you're in a corporate setting or a jet-setting serial entrepreneur.

I'm not trying to brag, but the feedback from these dealerships was phenomenal. The word got back to Detroit and the other plants that the ZJ project found the fix. Dealerships gave strong approval and validation for my prototype.

Dealership meetings lasted for just two days, and there was no time to wait to go into production mode. We spent another week for validation under an extreme heated environment, among a few other criteria. Once the finding was flawless and approved, Chrysler went ahead with production of the kits.

Time was scarce for assigning professional design teams and industrial designers to come up with an instruction manual for the kits. So, Chrysler senior management decided to use my written draft and visual work verbatim. This was the work that I had created with the design staff, who helped me during their non-peak business hours (probably out of pity and so that I would quit hounding them with phone calls several times a day). Next, Chrysler and Johnson Controls created an army of recall evangelists sent to the nooks and crannies of the world.

Despite the amount of drama involved, the entire recall saga lasted less than two months for me. I returned to Pitt to finish my senior year. Throughout senior year, I kept receiving emails and notes from my senior colleagues at Chrysler and Johnson Controls who traveled around the world to deliver training for the tool kit. The feedback was phenomenal, and the experience was humbling.

Before I knew it, my work was published, and I was invited to speak at some of the largest management conferences, including a key event within ANTEC Toronto. I heard through the grapevine that the total savings for Chrysler were in excess of $30-$40 million, and the project is still being considered an internal case study for managing recalls efficiently.

Sadly, Gary, someone I considered a mentor and who gave me enormous confidence to deal with difficult entrepreneurial challenges in life, was suffering silently from terminal cancer and passed away a few years later at the young age of 42.

As I finished my senior year, I received five job offers at various large corporations. I worked as director of R&D Design Center right out of school at Fortune 1000 Saint Gobain, Inc. in sunny California. At Saint Gobain, I successfully led yet another debut launching of a design center within the mega corporation. Saint Gobain was also great to me in terms of offering freedom and resources to spearhead the multimillion dollar design center, with direct reports that consisted of engineering, technicians, R&D personnel, and B2B salespeople.

I worked at Saint Gobain for two years, but this time around, it was different. It became difficult for me to sustain the same level of passion I once had at Chrysler. Daily corporate bickering and politics started to influence my creativity. I started feeling like millions of Americans working in corporate America. For me, my only motivation and excitement came from thinking like a startup. I had to get out of there.

Having gained unusually strong experience in corporate America during those couple of years, I left the company in 1999 to become an entrepreneur.

The late nineties were experiencing an entrepreneurial revolution with the dotcom bubble. Millions was being invested in ideas. "E-commerce" was the hot buzzword. I was in Southern California, home to the pioneers and venture capitalists, so I never looked back. I went on to start several companies in multiple verticals.

On the pages that follow, you'll read my story and the lessons I learned along the way.

What Will Conceptual Entrepreneurship Look Like?

"Every worthwhile accomplishment, big or little, has its stages of drudgery and triumph: a beginning, a struggle and a victory."
- Mahatma Gandhi, Political and Spiritual Leader

Not everybody is destined to be an entrepreneur.

Being an entrepreneur is not a get rich quick scheme.

Rudyard Kipling said it best in his poem, "If":

If you can dream - and not make dreams your master,
If you can meet with triumph and disaster
And treat those two imposters just the same
If you can make one heap of all your winnings
And risk it on one turn of pitch-and-toss,
And lose, and start again at your beginnings
And never breathe a word about your loss
Yours is the earth and everything that's in it.

No college degree or past accomplishment prepares you for the challenges that you will face as an entrepreneur. Your odds are obviously better if you are business savvy, have some form of business school background, and have some past entrepreneurial experience. Great entrepreneurs play smart and know when to quit and start all over again without hesitation.

In the conceptual generation, entrepreneurs have endless opportunities and tools, and smart entrepreneurs will try different options and move on to the one that yields the best results in the shortest turnaround time.

With the availability of custom software at your disposal (without having to learn a single line of codes) to the creative resources that you can acquire at $10-$20 per hour through websites like Elance.com and Odesk.com, creating a workable prototype has never been easier. Now, on your first presentation to a venture capitalist, you can actually take a working demo instead of a boring PowerPoint presentation like everybody else. The breakthroughs are not only in the areas of software, but also in areas such as entertainment, sports, biotechnology, green technology, and nanotechnology.

Nanotechnology is the future of science that will revolutionize the way materials and devices will be produced and manufactured. Since the foundation of the technology is based on molecular level production, we can only imagine how it will impact the processes, designs, and the economy.

Lower production costs will result in reduced operation costs, and that translates into lower costs of manufacturing, which will ultimately provide conceptual entrepreneurs with lower barriers to entry in terms of startup costs. I have summarized all of these new revolutionizing technologies throughout this book.

Entertainment is another big arena that will benefit heavily from the conceptual age. With the advent of digital filmmaking and inexpensive film editing software, a high school student can now do endless tricks with Final Cut Pro on his iMac, something that would have required a team in a larger production house 20 years ago.

We produced an original television series for entrepreneurs that aired nationally and on several Los Angeles stations. The shows were taped in professional studios, but the team that helped me put them together consisted of college and high school interns. I prefer to call them conceptual creative entrepreneurs.

I was skeptical in the beginning, but after successfully finishing taping of more than 20 shows in Hollywood and now continuing in Las Vegas, I wouldn't trade them for veteran staff. They are the future of moviemaking—the indie filmmakers of tomorrow!

On a larger scale, as digital security increases and the measures to tighten piracy mature, digital distribution of video content is going to improve drastically.

Green technology is not just another buzzword. The U.S. is in dire need of a solution for ongoing energy dependence on foreign oil. There is no time or room for politics to implement one and all measures ranging from wind, solar, and geothermal energy to drilling aggressively. All of these measures will create opportunities for conceptual entrepreneurs.

Regardless of the abundance in green opportunities, the challenges are not going to be menial. It is important for conceptual entrepreneurs not to fall into the clichéd mindset that new opportunities will bring easy money. A different set of opportunities will emerge, but the principle of entrepreneurship will remain the same. Each endeavor will require thoughtful analysis to determine if there actually is a market for the product or service that you are introducing and if potential customers consider the product/service of any value.

Having worked with more than 50 companies and CEOs of Fortune 500 companies and multinationals around the world, I will be the first one to tell you that entrepreneurship is one of the hardest things you will do in your life. You have to change your state of mind as well as have a killer product to make it in this ever more competitive environment. More often than not, you will fail, and most likely, you will fail miserably.

Andy Wilson, a venture capitalist based in Pasadena, who was behind the deal when Yahoo bought Overture for $1.7 billion, agreed with me that venture capitalists pass on hundreds of business plans before they decide to fund one. But when you are the chosen one or you make it, with or without a venture capitalist's help, it's the ultimate reward that you will experience.

Ten Critical Steps to Writing a Business Model For the Conceptual Age

"If I had eight hours to chop down a tree I would spend six hours sharpening my axe."
- Abraham Lincoln, 16th President of the United States

Starting a business is a major commitment that will consume 24/7 of your life with no end in sight. It's always good to know what you are getting into before you take the plunge. From my early years of experience creating business models, I have determined that there are basically two reasons why you need a business plan. The first is to reassure yourself that this wild dream you have in mind is attainable. The second reason is to convince a lender or venture capitalist to invest in your idea.

Whatever your reason may be, as the legendary management guru Peter Drucker would bluntly put it, "Always ask yourself what your business is, who your customers are, and what the customer considers value." In my opinion, here is a list of pointers that will save you many headaches.

Be Clear About What you're Selling. Spend as much time as you need to define and clarify what you are selling. From the get-go, come up with an elevator pitch with a clear value proposition. This will come in handy throughout the course of running your business. There are professional companies out there who can help you to discover who you are, what your company does, and what others perceive of you and your verbal and written messages.

Create a Proper Legal Structure For Your Business. Right legal structure will save you a lot of trouble later. There are many legal factors that come into play while choosing the right structure for your business. First, always consult a good business attorney. For instance, incorporating might cost you more in taxes with its double taxation clauses, but it will also provide you with the most immunity from personal liabilities.

Come Up with a Mission Statement, Vision Statement, and Objectives For Your Venture. They may all look the same at first glance, but they reflect different rationales. The mission statement represents the underlying operating philosophy and values of the company: "The mission at Company ABC is to provide a reliable, yet affordable XYZ technology for residential customers." The vision statement represents a long-term plan that provides a direction to make significant impact: "Our vision at company ABC is to become a global niche leader in XYZ technology by the year 2009." The objective represents definitive goals for different purposes within the company. Peter Drucker first popularized the term "management by objective" in his 1954 book, "The Practice of Management." Objectives can be set in all domains (services, sales, R&D, human resources, finances, etc.): "The main objective of company ABC is to understand the target market, implement the most optimized form of logistics, include a series of efficient fulfillment processes, and provide an unmatched form of customer service."

Be Honest About Your Strengths and Weaknesses. Conduct a simple SWOT analysis on your venture. SWOT stands for Strengths, Weaknesses, Opportunities, and Threats. Create four quadrants, and fill them up with honest answers. This simple test allows you to assess your compatibility with your venture. This test will also indicate opportunities, threats, and barriers to entry that exist in your vertical market.

Conduct Thorough Research on Your Vertical Market. Leverage new Internet research tools to conduct comprehensive studies. At every stage of your research, be open to adopting new directions based on your findings.

Make Sure This is a Real Opportunity, or move on to a different venture.

Make Sure Your Product or Service Addresses Pain Point(s). This goes back to understanding and addressing your customers' needs.

Conduct Thorough Research on Your Competitors. Create a matrix, and conduct a thorough competitive analysis. See what your competitors are offering.

Make Sure Your Product or Service Addresses Pain Point(s) *Better* **Than Your Competitors.** It's all right if your competitors got into the market before you, but focus on doing things a little bit differently. Address customer needs and pain points better than your competition.

Be Realistic with Revenue Projections. Don't fall into the trap of saying clichés like, "According to research, our market will be $X billion by ___" or "We will drop our product in China, and we will make billions." There is nothing wrong with wanting to become another Google or Microsoft, but make sure you have a unique product or service. If you have a patent on your innovation, that helps. If you already have an angel investor on board, that gives you credibility. If you have a veteran management team in place, that's going to help you a lot! Always be ready to explain to lenders and venture capitalists how you're going to reach the big numbers, and never ever use clichéd answers.

Surround Yourself with People Smarter Than You. Always reach out to people smarter than you. Big ideas take brilliant people to bring them to life. You want to do things intelligently and not give your idea away, but at the same time, you need to be open to sharing it with the right people. One rule of thumb is to team up with people with complementary skill sets. If you are an engineer, you don't need another engineer to support your point of view. You need a professional sales partner to sell your product and a sharp finance guy to keep the numbers in order.

Seize the Opportunity to Scale Up Quickly. Big deals don't happen on their own. Big deals happen because of right people, right product, and right momentum in the market among many possible variations. If you have everything in order, and luck is in your favor, seize the opportunity to scale up … and do it quickly! Otherwise, good entrepreneurs know when to pack up their bags and move on to another opportunity. I advise entrepreneurs to get out of the business if the venture doesn't take off within two years.

Winning Strategies for Entrepreneurs in the Conceptual Economy

"Business opportunities are like buses; there's always another one coming."
- Richard Branson, British Industrialist

I have been writing extensively on the conceptual economy, especially on how it will impact you whether you're an entrepreneur, a startup company, a thriving business, or an employee of a multinational corporation. It's critical to understand where you stand so that you can prepare yourself accordingly. As the legendary management guru Peter Drucker often said, "You cannot manage change; you can only stay ahead of it."

The New Role of Entrepreneurs in the Conceptual Economy

There are endless conceptual entrepreneurial opportunities. Never before in history have entrepreneurs had so much flexibility at their disposal. With the technology advancement and globalization of high speed connections, entrepreneurs have the power to do amazing things. This is welcoming news for knowledge entrepreneurs. Knowledge workers often had to rely on their parent organization or company to make a significant impact, which made it very hard to make it on their own.

These days, with the availability of modern tools, even college students can compete out of their dorm rooms with large multinationals. If you look at the recent history of innovation, numerous multinational companies were the result of college experiments at research labs and entrepreneurs' clubs. There are many great innovative groups out there such as the media lab at MIT and the MIT/Stanford Venture Lab. They exist in Europe, too, such as iConnect – INSEAD and London Business School Entrepreneurship Club.

As we all know, Facebook, Google, and eBay are some of the mega-household names that came out of academic settings. This is just the beginning. The level of success that eBay and Google experienced is few and far between, however. Still, the frequency of this kind of entrepreneurial success will grow exponentially in the future. Technologies are maturing, and the costs of technology are going down drastically due to healthy competition. Barrier to entry is going down. What the earlier Internet days promised prematurely is now becoming a reality. Virtual communities, portals, and social networking sites are already offering previews of what can be expected on the horizon.

The sky is the limit for conceptual entrepreneurs, and entrepreneurs have never liked to follow the rules anyway. This time around, they will truly get to lead the way in coming up with unique, yet surprisingly simple business models. The model that works in one geographic location may not work in another, but the beauty is that conceptual entrepreneurs will adapt (and they will adapt quickly).

Case in point: The way book publishing is taking place around the world is changing. A teenager in Japan wrote an entire novel, text messaging her content to her blog, and her fan readers downloaded portions at a time.

The concept became so popular that when the hard copy of her novel came out, it was an instant bestseller, and she made over $8 million. Believe it or not, half of the top ten books sold in Japan at the time were written by mobile phone authors. Japan is usually one of the first countries to adapt to new mobile technologies and concepts.

Some concepts translate to other cultures while the rest never transcend cultural differences. We may not see a cell phone novel on the New York Times Bestseller List anytime soon, but who knows? Some variation of the concept may catch on in the United States and Europe in the next decade.

Major publications have appropriately given importance to the rise of conceptual entrepreneurs. *The Wall Street Journal* recently started a feature section dedicated to entrepreneurs and regional accelerators.

Recognition and celebration of entrepreneurial culture in this manner means that conceptual entrepreneurs will get a platform for showcasing their ideas and improve their odds of making it.

I'm passionately involved in another fascinating national initiative called Startup America Partnership. This White House-launched, private sector-led initiative has been instrumental in fostering entrepreneurial ecosystems across the United States. Led by Internet pioneer, AOL chairman Steve Case and Priceline founder Scott Case, the group has expanded its presence to over 20 states and is still growing. I was involved in the California region's Startup California, and I'm leading the evolution of the neighboring Startup Nevada region.

Having been an entrepreneur with interest in multiple verticals, it has been an amazing experience working with conceptual entrepreneurs throughout the state of Nevada. I will be sharing some of the stories later in the book.

I consider the social media generation to be the first group to represent the conceptual generation. This generation is changing the way commerce is done and the way news is distributed. Big media is on board. More and more large networks are relying on user-generated content. Twitter has been a source of news unfolding in real time. Highly sophisticated mobile technologies have enabled regular folks to capture live footage and distribute it to their peers and the open world instantaneously.

Again, it's just the beginning. As the conceptual economy matures, technology will also mature and will open a platform for creativity and conceptual entrepreneurship to flourish.

In the conceptual economy, entrepreneurs will have tremendous capabilities to collaborate with resources from around the globe. Entrepreneurs will leverage each other beyond outsourcing menial tasks. This leveraging will be done on a scale and scope unheard of ever before in history.

Replicating ideas that work in one country, region, or vertical and taking it to other less developed markets is another concept that is catching on. Back in the day, eBay became very popular in the United States. Similar auction ideas mushroomed across the globe. In different segments of the market, local entrepreneurs initially started the wave, and once the concept became successful locally, their ventures were acquired by eBay for hefty sums.

The Indian version of eBay is called Bazee.com. It was acquired in 2004 for $50 million dollars. Similarly, eBay acquired iBazar, a French auction site, and Tradera, Sweden's leading online auction style marketplace.

In the world of social media, UBER is a creative new idea at its infant stage that lets passengers book their next car ride with a click on their smart phones. The initial response from UBER users was positive for this hassle-free, cashless form of car reservation. This strong indication led entrepreneurs in diverse verticals to apply this concept elsewhere.

Already, I have seen a version that they are trying for booking seats on private jets. Las Vegas-based Vegas Tech fund recently invested in another company that focuses on the hassle-free approach and the simple one-click payment method for ordering pizza. Only time will tell which one will make it in the long run.

In the conceptual generation, we will see this trend growing. There are enough entrepreneurial ideas and concepts floating around the world that conceptual entrepreneurs can and will easily tap into and convert to viable ventures.

As a factual note, America's Gross National Product has grown over the years, but the actual, physical weight of the GNP has declined. Go figure. This clearly supports the emergence of the new economic model.

Corporate Entrepreneurship: The Role of Management and Executives in the Conceptual Age

"Leadership must be respected, even though not loved. Make it happen and take responsibility. You can delegate authority, and still take responsibility. It is more important to be respected than to be loved. Leaders do not seek to be pleasing first."
- Gen. Norman Schwarzkopf

I was a student of Peter Drucker's at the Drucker School of Management. I followed his work for more than ten years. He often said that we cannot manage change, whether the change is in market demand, political climate, or a change in socioeconomic dynamics. We can and must sense the coming change and prepare to stay ahead of the curve.

With the current changing climate of the global sociopolitical landscape, this statement has never been more relevant.

Prior to adapting to Drucker's principles in management, large corporations like General Motors and General Electric had run on an industrial, labor-driven model instead of a knowledge-based structure. The knowledge economy that Drucker has contributed to in terms of principles has survived and operated effectively to this day. Well-run corporations learned to value knowledge workers and define roles of management in a way that benefitted the whole organization and the national economy.

As much as I commend and admire Drucker's economic and management model based on knowledge workers, the term that he famously coined, the time has come to rethink the roles of management and administrators both in the private and government sectors.

In the conceptual economy, the hierarchical management model might not be the most effective one. Corporate entrepreneurship should be the new mantra. It's becoming clearer that corporate America needs to increase innovation and entrepreneurial activities at every level within organizations. The culture of entrepreneurship is not only for individuals or startup ventures, but it should be for all corporations, small and large.

This culture also has a great place under the broad leadership of the army of middle managers across the corporate world. Middle managers are an often misunderstood segment of corporate America. You hear about jetsetting CEOs, or you come in contact with the company customer service rep, but you rarely hear about the tireless middle managers working behind the scenes. I can relate due to my only real job out of engineering school as a middle manager.

It was a blessing in disguise when I got that job. I learned that as a middle manager, you are stuck between a rock and a hard place. You are given a limited amount of decision-making capability from the top, and at the same time, you're constantly hounded by your reports about a never-ending cycle of smaller responsibilities. I call it a blessing because it was an opportunity to decide early on that entrepreneurship was my true calling. Looking back, I'm proud that I made that conscious choice, and hindsight turned out to be quite accurate in this case.

A growing amount of research is proving that middle managers can find themselves part of a dying breed unless they adapt to the new demands of the 21st century. I recently read a piece by London Business School professor Lynda Gratton on this topic, and she has firmly given an outlook of roles for middle managers in the future. She agrees with me that the old concept of knowledge jobs are gone for good.

Gone are the days when being a great craftsman and honing your craft could assure you a lifelong career. General management responsibilities at the middle management level are becoming less relevant.

Technology-enabled tools have replaced these tasks for middle managers, so they need to create sustainable competitiveness and create their value to salvage their positions in different ways. Like Gratton implies in her article, managers need to focus more on mentoring, fostering innovation, and entrepreneurship than managing daily tasks.

Middle managers need to be motivators and must play a supporting role in the broader scheme of creating a vision for the company. If done right, corporations will have an opportunity to let middle managers go free from their traditional roles and run more performance-driven, entrepreneurial ventures within the corporate setting. This can create tremendous morale among employees, as well as a tremendous opportunity for middle managers to constantly grow themselves. I'm sure we will hear more on corporate entrepreneurship at the middle manager level in the upcoming decade.

Gratton makes a great point that in the future, visibility for middle managers will not come from HR, but from peer-endorsed, peer-reviewed knowledge hubs. I agree.

In the conceptual economy, I would go one step further, however, and say that middle managers can also separate themselves from the herd by thinking like a startup community leader.

Startup community leaders do not have all the resources they need to launch a product, but they take the plunge anyway. Resourcefulness is what separates a good middle manager from a great one. Just like in the entrepreneurial world, middle managers are expected to deliver more with limited resources. Picking disciplined teams with entrepreneurial, innovative minds will be the key to performing tasks efficiently.

Morale is low among middle-level staff due to ambiguity and repetitiveness in the scope of projects they are assigned to complete. This kind of thing kills innovative spirit. The more playful and fun the environment can be made for middle-level workers, the more productivity will grow.

One company that is using the corporate entrepreneurship model well is Zappos. Las Vegas-based Zappos is a highly entrepreneurial workplace. Better known for its customer service than for the shoes it sells, Zappos encourages its staff to let loose, have fun, and adapt an entrepreneurial culture.

The company made a big move from San Francisco to downtown Las Vegas, and under the leadership of Tony Hsieh, the company encourages its staff to build an entrepreneurial culture. Zappos' customer service is so successful because of the ownership and passion that the entire staff shares for the company.

Customer support staff takes on the passion of an entrepreneur. Zappos directors encourage and facilitate staff members to start entrepreneurial ventures by offering training, resources, and other levels of support.

By making the entire staff entrepreneurial, Zappos has received many kudos for its superior customer service and as one of the best places to work.

In the conceptual economy, unless an old company adapts to new entrepreneurial norms within its organization, there will always be a lean company across the street, across town, across the country, or in another part of the world that's hungry and ready to snatch the market. This is the reality. If corporate America does not wake up and adapt the conceptual corporate entrepreneurship within its culture, the companies that stick to the old models will go the way of the dinosaur. It isn't a matter of if; it's a matter of when.

These are some of the measures that corporations can take to make their workforce entrepreneurial:

A. With direct guidance from upper management, middle managers should set up a sub-entrepreneurial culture in the workplace and keep HR completely out of the picture.

B. The lower level workforce should be given a sense of ownership by not micromanaging, but allowing flexibility and measuring performance based on individual contribution, as well as based on a broader level of impact that individuals make to the whole community (respective departments).

C. Collaborative culture should be brought to both intra and inter-departments. Each department should be viewed as a venture in an entrepreneurial ecosystem. Just like in the real world the way ventures die if they do not work with other members of the entrepreneurial ecosystem, individual departments can bring down the whole organization if they don't work together. This is a good time to revisit intra and inter-departmental competitive models that were traditionally used to boost productivity.

D. In the conceptual economy, we need to rethink how non-profit organizations are run, encouraging charities to take risks and become more aggressive toward growth. The conceptual economy will help create an atmosphere for non-profit leaders to have the same level of risk-taking freedom that for-profit enterprises have enjoyed in the knowledge economy.

After all of these decades, Peter Drucker is still relevant in terms of his comment that the purpose of a business is to create a customer. And in the conceptual economy, you attain this goal by being inclusive, collaborative, and providing a return for the community at different levels.

Unbiased Connectivity: The Vegas Tech and Nevada Entrepreneurial Ecosystem

"Logic will get you from A to B. Imagination will take you everywhere."
- Albert Einstein, Theoretical Physicist

Many people around the world don't consider Las Vegas the technology or entrepreneurial capital of the world. It's known as probably the most recognizable gaming and vacation destination in the world, and it boasts the world's largest, most extravagant casinos and event centers. Conventions like CES (International Consumer Electronics Show), NAB (National Association of Broadcasters), and CTIA Wireless collectively bring in over a quarter of a million visitors to these events annually.

But things are changing in Vegas, and they're changing quite fast. I have seen a small group of entrepreneurs working hard to build a viable tech and entrepreneurial community there in a relatively short period of time.

Unfortunately, I saw comments on Twitter undermining the effort. This attitude is changing for the right reasons, however. The Vegas Tech community is growing steadily because of the strong dedication of the members who are committed to make it happen.

The Las Vegas community has been very supportive of this initiative. Local corporations like Zappos and SWITCH have been sponsoring events, ranging from organizing notable entrepreneurial speaker series to sponsoring the Vegas Tech group's attendance at national events like SXSW in Austin, Texas.

Vegas Tech is also getting a lot of credibility as the early backer Downtown Project has set aside $50 million for community-based, socially-conscious entrepreneurial companies. This is encouraging entrepreneurs from across the United States, as well as across the pond, to migrate to Vegas. The Downtown Project and Vegas Tech are leveraging organizations like Venture for America and Startup America Partnership to bring young, aspiring entrepreneurs to the city. Vegas Tech is also working with local incubators SciTech and The Innevation Center to organize various events to foster entrepreneurial ecosystems and clusters in the state.

As a result of the common spirit of this entrepreneurial collaboration, Vegas Tech members are pushing every day to foster the local entrepreneurial scene.

The goal of the Downtown Project is to offer startup capital to entrepreneurs and companies that strictly believe in fostering the downtown community. The idea is noble, considering that entrepreneurship can be driven individualistically and that Vegas Tech and the Downtown Project in general fosters entrepreneurs starting businesses and living in downtown Las Vegas.

This initiative is receiving tremendous support from the city, and the interest is being felt in other parts of the state. Vegas Tech has created a sense of pride among Nevadans who love to see the non-gaming economy grow.

By the time this book comes out, it's likely that the Vegas Tech entrepreneurial ecosystem will have grown even stronger. In the conceptual economy, the key to sustainable growth will have a lot to do with letting the Vegas Tech community grow organically. Unbiased support from the founding backers and an ongoing unbiased connectivity between cities, small and large alike, are crucial.

Medicine and the Conceptual Economy

"Success is walking from failure to failure with no loss of enthusiasm."
- Winston Churchill, British Politician

The knowledge economy saw tremendous progress in the world of medicine. With the maturity of industrial discipline came a series of modern day innovations and best practices in medicine. Medical doctors and technologists received a prestigious status as knowledge workers, which led to secure careers and prestige in the knowledge economy. Though the scale of progress, especially in the western world, was noteworthy, it will be no match for what we are about to witness in the conceptual economy.

The speed of innovation will grow exponentially. The knowledge economy saw growth in a linear fashion, and disruption took place in a periodic, predictable way. In the conceptual economy, there will be multiple disruptions in a complementary fashion, in intra and inter-verticals at the same time. Conceptual entrepreneurs will need to adapt quickly. There will be many opportunities, but challenges will follow each step.

Again, barrier to entry for innovators will diminish significantly, but sustaining relevance and competiveness will require a correct dose of science, art, and an understanding of human behavior.

Patients will have access to tools that will enable them to take full control over the welfare of their health. The era has already begun where patients can self-quantify and monitor various conditions.

I recently met the executive producers of the non-profit Singularity University, a learning institution based in Silicon Valley. The mission of the organization is to "assemble, educate and inspire a cadre of leaders who strive to understand and facilitate the development of exponentially advancing technologies and apply, focus and guide these tools to address humanity's grand challenges."

The mission statement was quite fitting, as I had a chance to review their recently organized seven-day event called "FutureMed." It would be an understatement to say that the participants at this event were an optimistic bunch. I personally knew two of the participants this year representing Maine and Nevada. They came in from all around the world for this jam-packed gathering.

Here are some of the people, ideas, and wisdom presented at the event that I found fascinating.

In recent history, the venture capital industry is losing interest in medicine, seeing it as high risk. Though investments by venture capitalists have gone down by as much as two-thirds in the last few years, there is a whole new group of angel investors investing in similar amounts to a larger pool of startups who prefer companies that adapt innovations, reduce costs, approach problems in unique and cost-effective ways, and provide clear return on investment.

For an innovator or a wannabe conceptual entrepreneur, this is a great time to launch a venture or pursue an entrepreneurial career.

The conceptual economy will demand that entrepreneurs think outside of the box. Todd Brinton of Stanford BioDesign has launched a 12-month fellowship program. Todd pointed out at the FutureMed event that too often, people try to jam technologies into a need instead of building technologies to fit a need.

Selected fellows in his program spend six months researching and working on the needs, and the remaining six months inventing and implementing solutions.

Tim O'Reilly of O'Reilly Media pointed out that in the new (conceptual) economy, new systems will get better if more people use them. These days, hackers of the world and open source platforms are the new R&D.

I agree fully with O'Reilly. In the conceptual economy, it will only get harder for individual corporations and research labs to do the hard lifting on their own. As I have indicated in other parts of the book, the old competitive forces model will become less relevant moving forward as the world moves toward the collaborative model.

Executives from the pharmaceutical industry attended another session, and according to the Singularity blog entry, they tend to agree. These pharma executives say that clinical trials are costing too much with failure rates getting worse. The pharmaceutical companies that they represent are starting to collaborate with non-pharma medical companies that focus on selling outcomes rather than medications. This model has been productive and, most likely, will continue to escalate in the conceptual economy.

Conceptual entrepreneurs who see this opportunity can adapt to new models based on these tips and keep trying to make the old model work. When paradigm shifts occur in industries, conceptual entrepreneurs should learn to adapt instead of going against the tide of change.

Another interesting initiative going on to catalyze research in cancer genomes is a cancer genomes browser. Open source initiatives like this make data public and help to create a collaborative atmosphere.

In the new economy, doctors are going to have access to amazing tools. One of these is the rapid advent of 3D printing. Using this technology, your neighborhood dentist can print replacement teeth onsite while you wait, or a surgeon can touch and feel a replica body organ prior to performing an invasive surgery. My brother is an orthopedics surgeon, and I have seen firsthand inside the operation theater the challenges that doctors go through because they don't have enough data to make right calls in the moment.

Beyond 3D printing, innovations are everywhere in the world of medicine. Another non-invasive technique in genetics is fitting for the conceptual thinking. This technique in neuroscience uses light to switch nerves on and off, offering a non-invasive cure for nerve diseases, including a cure for hypertension.

There have been some major breakthroughs in non-invasive medicine. According to Peter Altman from BioCardia, there will be a shift from systemic (accessing the body either through pill or vein) to molecular targeting using nano-enabled devices.

Nano medicine will also play a major role in designing red cells. Nano technology will enable manufacturing atoms in 3D and will enable a much higher quality of healthcare while also bringing costs down.

There have also been some major developments in brain to Bionics integration, wearable robotics, artificial retina and DNA sequencing, and genome medicine.

Another great resource that conceptual thinkers and entrepreneurs will have is artificial intelligence within technology platforms and social media. Artificial intelligence will amplify innovation in the conceptual economy. Broader artificial intelligence in an open-source, social media setting will offer a platform and better hypotheses for many innovative, collaborative opportunities.

This is a great chance for entrepreneurs, scientists, and innovators to leverage multiple paradigm shifts by building innovations that address the pain points of the patients. Like Todd Brinton said: Building technologies to fit the need rather than trying to jam technologies into a need.

Local Nevada Connections

As I indicated in my first chapter, the new economy will demand that entrepreneurs and innovators think differently. It took half a century to define knowledge workers and the knowledge-based jobs they performed. In the earlier days, management was pure art and not a formal area of study. The need to structure workflow and governance to lead large organizations led to modern day management consultants. These consultants introduced best practices in all verticals, and they established processes from organization-wide performance evaluation and Enterprise resource planning to supply chain management to quantifying and analyzing sustainable competitive forces.

Michael Porter, Harvard professor and strategy god of the knowledge economy, became a poster child for the success story in corporate strategy and protective corporate culture. Porter's competitive forces model made him the darling of Fortune 500 CEOs. Heads of states of sovereign nations started to seek consulting from him and his private management consulting practices. Companies started to analyze ways to stay ahead of the game, understand the competition, and control competitors before they would become a threat. Porter's model further analyzed the ways that an organization could stay ahead of the pack by understanding and leveraging suppliers, partners, and intra-organizational ecosystems.

This kind of thinking went really well for most mega-corporations. But the overall competitive nature of this model started getting a backlash as big companies and entrepreneurs started to miss out on opportunities by sticking too close to the competitive forces model and not being adaptive enough to a more collaborative model. In many instances, it became apparent that there is not much to protect if the fundamental paradigm is shifting or customers are leaving in droves.

In the case of sovereign developing nations, protecting the little they had became less productive in the long run compared to opportunities from collaboration and resource sharing (concepts rarely used in the knowledge economy).

Conceptual leaders will emerge from all walks of life and industry verticals. Dr. Chandler Marrs is a Las

Vegas-based leader who is dedicated to fostering entrepreneurship in the biomedical vertical. I recently sat down with her to discuss in detail a possible collaboration between her initiative and the nano-technology field that I am exploring.

What Dr. Marrs is doing for the Nevada economy can be considered an example of how a solo creative conceptual entrepreneur can emerge in the next couple of decades. I met her for the first time as a fellow panelist on the White House's Council on Jobs and Competitiveness. I had several correspondences with her after that meeting. In each encounter, I saw her as an entrepreneur who truly cares about her local entrepreneurial communities and pushes her non-profit mission to build a world-class biomedical cluster in Southern Nevada. She currently runs a 501(c)(3) Parallel Innovation Lab in Henderson, working to make it a dedicated incubator for science entrepreneurs. Beginning last year, she also started the first SciTech Hookup, a collaborative conference for science entrepreneurs and Nevada-based resources to network and launch startups. At last year's event, leaders of established biomedical clusters from major U.S. cities attended to lend their support.

The one aspect that fascinated me was that she has a for-profit venture related to women's hormone issues that she rarely talks about. She is so passionate about communal causes that she hesitates to be an entrepreneur and push for her own startup

It's taking some time to launch her company, Lucine Biomedical, which is still in the alpha mode, but in the new economy, a company like Lucine will be successful eventually because there is a strong support system from the camaraderie Dr. Marrs has built in the non-profit arena.

She is working on creating a platform to collect hormone-related data in an easy-to-use online application, where women can upload their symptoms, irregularities, and complications and be given useful information. This platform will eventually support entrepreneurs to come up with cures and innovative treatments.

I have been following Dr. Marrs' research since my mother has been suffering from undiagnosed hormone-related complications for the last ten years. Every day, my mother has suffered from undiagnosed complications that have affected the quality of her life significantly. As I am finding out concretely through Dr. Marrs' research, there is a scarcity in the research data for offering a proper diagnosis, and this impacts half a billion people around the world.

I'm happy to think that the future outlook is brighter. In the knowledge economy, doctors were trained with "inside the box" mentality. Research data was scarce and non-collaborative, and open platform research was non-existent. This led to medical treatments with limited subject matter research, often leading to massive side effects like in the case of my mother.

Hormone study is going to be one of many lines of research that will impact the way researchers in the conceptual economy will share and collaborate on data to come up with better products in a relatively shorter period of time. How will this impact the consumption of hormone therapy drugs? How will this self-awareness and self-monitoring of the patient's own well-being help people to self-diagnose their symptoms or at least attempt to explore suitable solutions to make their daily lives more tolerable?

Dr. Marrs intends to collect a sample pool via her private company and open source platforms by educating the masses and bringing awareness via social media platforms like Twitter and Facebook. Collection of enough data, in this case or in any other health field for that matter, will lead to useful information for scientists looking for cures. Adequate research samples in a collaborative setting could help conceptual science entrepreneurs come up with business models that could lead to finding the right drugs or developing drug delivery systems enabled by new technologies like nano technology.

I am passionately exploring nano technology and finding ways to collaborate with science entrepreneurs, venture capitalists, and angel investors to explore its short-term and long-term implications and benefits. I studied engineering in the area of polymer science, so my subject matter expertise is in the materials side.

The future of nano technology can be categorized into the two segments of materials and devices. Nano technology has hugely impacted the materials arena by finding ways to make materials stronger, more durable, and more flexible. Practical applications of nano technology were seen as early as the late nineties, and the technology was pioneered at nano research-focused schools like Pittsburg State University, my alma mater. Research in this field will only get bigger in the upcoming decades.

Another segment of nano technology is in devices. The secret sauce of nano technology is that science is in nano-scale. Using this technology, you can make devices smaller and more efficient with better conductive properties than in the past. The analogy can be loosely drawn with the early rise of the semi-conductor industry that led to the technology revolution that is still going strong today.

Another powerful application will be in the world of medical devices. Imagine the possibilities when you can deliver drugs using nano devices, while another set of nano devices can go inside the human body and fix blood cells. Because of the scale, nano medical devices can do wonders for the future of modern medicine.

Let's talk about how all of this will impact conceptual entrepreneurs like you. How can you benefit or add value to launch scale ventures in this field? The answer is simple. As Drucker would put it back in the day, nobody can foresee the future; you can only be ready when the opportunity comes knocking on your door.

And the opportunities in nano, as well other new fields, could be endless. Imagine nano-based manufacturing companies in which products will be developed at a molecular level. Talk about disruptive! There will be a whole new workforce required at every step. We are not only talking about knowledge workers like scientists, researchers, and lab analysts. Try to imagine how the manufacturing vertical will be redefined. Who will be your suppliers in your nano company? Who will be your customers? How will the distribution channel look at the Business to Consumer (B2C) level? What kind of models will emerge out of commercial nano applications?

Will pharmaceutical companies adapt to the new technology, or will we have to wait until the existing medical device industry is phased out? How will the non-invasive aspect of nano medical devices impact highly invasive surgeries? What will happen to the medical institutes equipped to conduct surgery if they find out that non-invasive surgery is far safer and costs only a fraction of what it would cost for traditional surgery? What happens to medical institutions teaching traditional invasive medicine? Will they adapt quickly enough to develop subject matter experts in their states, or will the disruptive model be tested elsewhere first?

What will the new regulations look like? Will government catch up with the technology quickly, or will the technology take the lead in an open, collaborative platform with governments playing catch up late in the game? What will ethical compliance look like? How will this technology help or hurt sensitive areas of governance? How will the equal playing field in terms of modern technology affect regional competitiveness? Who will come out as leaders? What will medical courses look like in academic settings?

And now, imagine all of the possibilities for entrepreneurs in every one of these areas. We have no clue what the jobs of tomorrow will look like, but we know it will be very different. And being "disruptive" will be the normal vocabulary for entrepreneurs.

Now, think about today. The science fiction nano days will come, but there are some areas of nano which are already real, like the ones I mentioned earlier in the fields of materials, semiconductors, and medical delivery. How can you make an impact by taking a pragmatic approach?

Conceptual Entrepreneurs Will Come From All Walks of Life

I joined Twitter back in 2008 when it was still in its infancy. One person I noticed on Twitter in those early days was a local CBS newscaster based in Las Vegas, Dave Courvoisier. I could tell right away that he was a creative conceptual entrepreneur, and he used Twitter frequently. The only time he seemed to not be on Twitter was while he was on the air. Dave actively marketed his various creative entrepreneurial ventures on his Twitter feed.

Fast forward to 2013, and now that I have one of my offices based in Vegas, I see Dave on the local CBS Channel 8. He is still active on Twitter, sharing information about his company, but now, he also markets his television station, giving a heads up on the upcoming stories on the evening news.

With the advent of innovative real time social media tools like Twitter, local newscasters like Dave no longer need to rely on their studios to do all the marketing for them, and television stations no longer need to rely entirely on their marketing and sales teams to get the word out. While Dave is actively promoting his voiceover acting services, he is also marketing the station that he works for. He provides the times that he will be on the air for the totally new demographics on these new media like Twitter. These are demographics that typically would not watch the local news.

Dave is a great example of somebody who is using this social medium properly. Traditionally, television has been a one-to-many medium with news fed in one direction. Viewers have limited ways to interact with their favorite television personalities. Now, while the traditional role of television is still relevant, members of the news business can actively participate with their viewers, giving a glimpse of what to expect in the evening news ahead of time. So, in a way, viewers can pull their local news and watch only certain segments that interest them, avoiding annoying noise.

Perception of social media tools like Twitter has improved drastically over the years. In the earlier days, Twitter was often wrongly perceived as a tool that only people with a lot of free time would use for mundane updates.

I wrote about the arrival of the shift and mentioned in a 2009 blog post that Twitter represented the arrival of a new form of communication. I argued that Twitter complemented traditional media and did not threaten to replace them. The arrival of the Twitter business model represents one of the few moments in the history of media that qualifies as a revolution.

I agree with what Clay Shirky said in his TED presentation that there were four periods in the last 500 years when the media model changed enough to qualify as a revolution. These are (1) the printing press in the middle 14th century, (2) the arrival of two-way conversational media some 200 years ago (first, the text-based telegraph followed by the voice-based telephone), (3) the arrival of recorded media that came in the form of photos, recorded sound, television, and movies in the early 1900s, and (4) the arrival of the Internet.

Historically, all media revolutions enhanced communication between people whether it was one-to-one (telegram, telephone) or one-to-many (television). In the case of the Internet, the impact has been exponentially larger because of its unique capacity to reach masses in a revolutionary many-to-many format. Even though the Internet provides that platform, applications like Twitter (and in my opinion, at this time, Twitter is the only company that understands this model well) enable individuals and businesses to practice this concept.

How often can you communicate with 5,000 people on your network instantaneously? Email is effective, but Twitter takes many-to-many communication to the next level. Unlike email, people on your Twitter network have already opted in, so most likely, your message is received well among like-minded people. You can hear from them instantaneously as well, truly focusing on the message rather than focusing on the medium.

By the way, I got my first invitation for a national television appearance in the form of a tweet. I am a strong believer in adding value. As long as Twitter adds value to its users, a moneymaking business model will emerge. Twitter is a great conceptual age business that offers a valuable tool for its users.

Unbiased Connectivity and Building Ecosystems

"It is amazing what you can accomplish if you do not care who gets the credit."
- Harry S. Truman

Since May of 2012, I have been helping Startup America Partnership as a region champion to launch the Nevada region. Living in Los Angeles, I traveled to Las Vegas on numerous occasions for leisure. Gaming dominates the Nevada economy and is the main job provider in the state, but as I mentioned earlier, this economic model is changing. There are crops of new entrepreneurial ecosystems emerging throughout the state.

I was friends with some of the leading social entrepreneurs in California, who were actively pushing to launch Startup California, a regional affiliate of Startup America Partnership, the White House-launched initiative to foster entrepreneurial ecosystems. I supported their cause and thought it was a great initiative to nurture entrepreneurship in often ignored communities who are not blessed with the same caliber of experts and investors that you would find in entrepreneurial super hubs like Silicon Valley. It was recommended that I take the lead in Nevada as a region champion. Hence, I transplanted to Nevada in mid-2012. It seemed like a sudden move to Nevada, but the journey has turned out to be quite interesting. I have had a chance to learn a great deal from entrepreneurs and leaders who are older, as well as younger, than I am. I met young Nevada entrepreneurial leaders along the way, who returned to their small Nevada home towns to take the lead in establishing local entrepreneurial hubs.

Daniel Herr is a great example of a bright Reno-based entrepreneur who attended Cornell and returned to his hometown. I came to know of him through his colleague at NIREC, a non-profit organization in the renewable energy sector, at the annual National Eco Summit in Las Vegas. A colleague of Dan at NIREC indicated that Dan was working on building a local entrepreneurial ecosystem in Reno and was interested in helping with Startup Nevada.

I visited Reno the following week for what turned out to be a great meeting with Daniel and other local entrepreneurs. This was also a great time for me to learn about entrepreneurship in small town America. I was passionate about helping to build an inter-city entrepreneurial ecosystem. I was already familiar with emerging ecosystems in the Las Vegas area like the one led by Tony Hseih and Zappos. I thought it would be a great opportunity to facilitate a connection between entrepreneurs in different cities.

Being an entrepreneur is tough and often an isolated experience as you deal with situations on your own. At times, tasks seem monumental without any concrete solutions in sight. But if done right, there is no better high than being a successful entrepreneur.

Twentieth century America saw solo entrepreneurs or entrepreneurs in small groups leading the way, building major corporations like Microsoft, Apple, and Xerox, to name a few. Those small groups of well-connected individuals leveraged the emerging concept of venture capital and built enterprises that were previously thought to be impossible. The number of venture funds grew, and so did the pool of younger connected entrepreneurs wanting to leverage venture funds. As a larger percentage of the workforce became motivated to become entrepreneurs, the dynamics of raising capital and the competitive landscape also started to change.

A pragmatic approach to entrepreneurship became overshadowed by the hype and easy moneymaking schemes. The term "entrepreneur" got a bad reputation and was used loosely to refer to unemployed individuals just looking to make a quick buck.

So, movements like Startup America, Startup Weekend, and other privately owned incubators are welcomed with open arms as these movements support and show the ropes to budding entrepreneurs. Ecosystems are perfect places to nurture entrepreneurship in the right way. As an entrepreneur, I can say firmly that it takes a village. Actually, in the modern scenario, it takes an entire city, state, region, and the whole nation to raise an entrepreneur.

Ecosystems provide entrepreneurs with an environment to grow. They need a balance of individuals, however, including mentors, venture capitalists, angel investors, and the type of governance that celebrates entrepreneurship culture.

The Las Vegas Downtown Project is an example of what works in a public-private partnership. With companies like Zappos and other regional private companies taking the lead and with active support from the city of Las Vegas, there is a major revitalization effort right now. The development effort and all the improvements that are taking place are noteworthy and could be an example to follow for other downtown areas.

The Downtown Project has set aside $350 million for various downtown-related projects, setting aside $50 million for the Vegas Tech Fund. Vegas Tech Fund prefers investing in startups with a culture that fosters a sense of community.

I met with the founders of Bluefields.com, a London-based startup, a 500 Startups graduate, and a recent recipient of the Vegas Tech Fund investment, who are building an event management platform. Bluefields is the kind of community building and community conscious company that Vegas Tech is interested in. Companies like Bluefields help ecosystems like downtown Las Vegas become a great platform for conceptual entrepreneurs.

In order for communities like downtown Las Vegas to thrive in a sustainable way, there needs to be ongoing unbiased connectivity. While I, along with executives and young MBA students around the globe, admire the work of strategy gurus like Michael Porter, competitive models need to be revisited. If we are too focused on protecting rather than collaborating and growing, we will be destined for failure. These days, communities do not flourish on their own. Entrepreneurs need to take the higher road and choose collaboration over competition, at least during their early startup years. Some of the best creative ideas will be fostered via collaboration, getting people with complementary skill sets involved in the value creation process.

I see this process unfolding in a constructive fashion in the city of Las Vegas. The Downtown Project has started a speakers' series where notable speakers, renowned entrepreneurs, and subject matter experts come to town and speak exclusively for entrepreneurs working in the downtown ecosystem. Producers of Singularity University were among the speakers.

Leading doctors, scientists, and engineers attend the various events that Singularity University organizes annually to learn to become conceptual entrepreneurs and to find collaborators to launch disruptive ideas. Singularity has successfully partnered with networks from around the world for leading drug research and technology co-development in an expedited, less bureaucratic fashion.

NIREC-sponsored Project Vesto is another great example that is promoting entrepreneurship by organizing one of the largest business plan competitions in the world with a prize of $100,000. The competition is being co-financed by the Nevada Governor's office and local Nevada-based private investors. Approximately 200 contestants submitted their plans from throughout the state in what is turning out to be a very successful entrepreneurial outreach effort, and I'm honored to be invited as one of the judging panelists.

The entrepreneurial spirit created by the contestants who will be pitching to the team of judges is priceless. One venture will walk away with $100,000, but the remaining participants will walk away with a drive to make their ventures even bigger. It's the kind of spirit that pushes entrepreneurial communities to the next level.

There are many capital sources out there for conceptual entrepreneurs in every state in the union. I have a strong wish that people reading this book will not walk away with just specific resources to raise money or market their ideas, however. I sincerely hope that you will walk away knowing that the sky is the limit and that there are countless ways you can add value to your entrepreneurial ventures and make your entrepreneurial journey sustainable.

Having said that, let's define what "value add" means in the conceptual economy. If you have ever done sales or been part of a business course, "adding value" almost becomes a cliché. So, let's put it in laypersons' terms. A pragmatic approach to adding value involves addressing the pain points of your customers or potential customers. Adding value means complementing the skill set(s) that your organization might need. Adding value means that you are doing something differently so that the end user experience is friendlier. It means you are solving the same problems, but you are being more creative and making it even more user-friendly.

From an even bigger picture, adding value is giving back to the society that nurtured you; it's helping fellow entrepreneurs who are trying to follow in your footsteps. It's about mentoring aspiring entrepreneurs. I cannot emphasize enough the true importance and value of giving back.

I have been fortunate to be able to help thousands of entrepreneurs via the blogs and television shows that I have created in the last seven years. I have also been fortunate to be able to find some of the coolest collaborative opportunities along the way. My intention, though, was not to make a single dime out of these hundreds of posts, columns, and over 20 television shows that I produced and hosted. It gives me tremendous joy when I am led to be part of cutting-edge companies or to be part of a producing feature film team that made it to the prestigious Berlin Film Festival. It's an honor to get to know such truly remarkable entrepreneurs like yourself.

So, the next time you think of ways to truly add value, dig down to your inner value system. Ask yourself why you do what you do and why you do it passionately. Value propositions may not always be clear, but you can come up with a unique proposition that reflects you and/or your organization. Always make "giving back" a part of your value-proposition. And when it comes to giving back to the community you care about, make it an unbiased act without wanting anything in return.

Crowdfunding

"Entrepreneurship is neither a science nor an art. It is a practice."
- Peter Drucker

At some point or another, every entrepreneur has experienced scarcity of capital. Not having access to capital can paralyze an operation in a heartbeat. The 2008 economic downturn made things even worse in the capital market, and banks are not releasing funds for small companies. Banks played a role more as asset manager than entrepreneur-friendly risk taker. The same can be said about many venture capital and institutional funds across the United States today. These institutional investors have deep pockets but are very picky as to the frequency and size of their investments. Bright minds are hired to manage assets, and safe bets are usually made instead of truly taking chances on out-of-the-box entrepreneurial ideas and optimism.

The tremendous growth in the American economy can be traced to earlier prominent venture capitalists like Perkins Kleiners and Sequoia, which took enormous chances on entrepreneurial optimism and invested in mere ideas. Intel Corporation's hastily typewritten one-page business summary indicates the trust that venture capitalists in those early days placed on these entrepreneurial ventures.

Eugene Kleiner created Kleiner Perkins, one of the most successful venture capital firms known for backing ventures like Google, Sun Microsystems, Amazon, and AOL. Kleiner was known for his business wisdom often referred to as "Kleiner's Laws."

Here are some of his quotes:

- "Make sure the dog wants to eat the dog food. No matter how groundbreaking a new technology, how large a potential market, make sure certain customers actually want it."

- "Build one business at a time. Most business plans are overly ambitious. Concentrate on being successful in one endeavor first."

- "The time to take the tarts is when they're being passed. If an environment is right for funding, go for it." (Kleiner, more than anyone, knew that venture capital goes in cycles.)

- "The problem with most companies is that they don't know what business they're in."

- "Even turkeys can fly in a high wind. In times of strong economies, even bad companies can look good."

- "It's easier to get a piece of an existing market than to create a new one."

- "It's difficult to see the picture when you're inside the frame."

- "After learning some of the tricks of the trade, some people think they know the trade." (This reflected some of Kleiner's own humility; he recognized that many venture capitalists thought they were experts when they had just a bit of knowledge.)

- "Venture capitalists will stop at nothing to copy success."

- "Invest in people, not just products."

Kleiner always respected founding entrepreneurs. He wanted to build companies with them, not just with their ideas.

In those earlier days, visionaries like Kleiner played crucial roles in laying out the rules. Many of the investors and venture capitalists who followed Kleiner followed his wisdoms. Back in the day, it was important for a handful of forward-thinking institutional investors to take the lead. But times have changed.

The conceptual economy is seeing rapid, easy access to information and knowledge. With the fast commercialization of the Internet toward the end of the last century and now social media taking center stage, individual small-time investors have access to the same caliber of knowledge that was enjoyed only by the privileged elite investors in the past.

Changes in regulation are also needed in terms of how individual investors can invest in the companies that they have been following in the news or the ones started by their neighbors or grandkids. Easy access to information means having access to tools that will enable individual investors to make decisions about their investments.

The Kickstarter model is a great example of how entrepreneurs are raising enormous sums of money to build products that they would not have been able to raise via traditional lenders, investors like banks, angel investors, or venture capitalists. I was a part of the producing team for a feature film called "Highway." In 2011, we were successful in raising over $30,000 within a few days via Kickstarter. The movie was already complete before it was posted on Kickstarter, but this extra money allowed us to take the post-production and marketing to the next level and also garner tremendous support from Hollywood star power. In 2012, "Highway" was nominated for the main line-up in the prestigious 2012 Berlin International Film Festival, which opened doors for worldwide commercial distribution.

Creative professionals in the past were often associated as freelancers working on a project. By nature, creative types had to rely on larger clients such as advertising agencies and movie production houses for those projects. Very few freelancers were successful in starting big ventures in the world of entertainment and music.

In the conceptual economy, creative freelancers can truly be conceptual entrepreneurs and tackle large projects. This works because today, an individual's original creative work can be found and seen through many avenues. An independent filmmaker no longer needs the marketing resources of a big production house to put his/her work out into the market.

Another beauty of the conceptual economy is that less content will be pushed, and more content will be specifically pulled by viewers, listeners, columnists, critics, and laypeople so that good content will find a home.

In order for you as an entrepreneur to succeed in this "pull-based" economy, the most important preparation is to come up with an online personality that reflects who you are, what you do, and what you are looking for.

The Smart Way of Working: The End of the Knowledge Economy as We Know It

"All achievements, all earned riches, have their beginning in an idea."
- Napoleon Hill

Last year, I connected with Bruce Rosenstein, a notable author and veteran *USA Today* writer for 21 years. He is the author of "Living in More Than One World: How Peter Drucker's Wisdom Can Inspire and Transform Your Life." As we were sharing personal anecdotes about Peter Drucker, I reflected on the profound influence that Drucker had on leaders and followers alike. With his humble approach, vast knowledge, wide contribution, and voracious appetite for management writing, his influence can be seen in the nooks and crannies of the world.

I also felt speaking to Rosenstein was a great opportunity for me to reflect on my own journey in life and on the way some of the best business leaders of the 20th century directly influenced me. I rarely focus on my personal stories, but I feel it's time for me to open up and share my values and the knowledge that I have gained over the years.

I have had incredible opportunities to work with some of the greatest minds and personalities in the world and help build several successful enterprises along the way. As of this writing, my enterprises have created jobs for more than 500 individuals, and I strongly intend to scale. I'm also deeply influenced by the situational leadership style of Douglas Conant, the past CEO of Campbell's.

I had a humble childhood within an extremely strong and educated family environment in Kathmandu, Nepal. Growing up, I attended St. Xaviers Catholic boarding school run by Jesuit fathers. It was an environment extremely suited to individualism and "the sky is the limit" dialogue. Later on, it fit into the notion of "American Exceptionalism," allowing me to have the confidence and the right knowledge to contribute in the United States today. As a teen, when I moved to a small, affluent town in mid-Ohio, my early strong values stayed with me.

Wooster, Ohio is a small town in America nestled between Cleveland and Cincinnati. The economically strong town had a population of 20,000 broadly representing upper middle class demographics. The well-known plastics company, Rubbermaid, was started in this town as an entrepreneurial family venture, and to this day, it's one of the largest corporations run with home-grown values. Stanley Gault was the iconic CEO who ran the ship for decades.

Some time during my first year in Wooster, I had a chance meeting with Gault through a family friend, Brenda Franks, at a local Wal-Mart store. That same year, Rubbermaid was named most admired company by *Fortune* magazine. That meeting changed my perspective on entrepreneurship and forever influenced the way I formed and sustained enterprises.

Stanley Gault's influence stayed with me even several years later when I helped Chrysler Corporation with their multimillion dollar recall project. As much as I was impressed at Chrysler with the surroundings of the big three corporate culture and eventually elated by my success there, I was also distracted by the inefficiencies, redundant processes, and dwindling quality of auto-making and manufacturing. Over the following years, my interest grew sharply toward looking for ways to run enterprises more efficiently. I wanted to fundamentally rethink corporate management and leadership styles for the emerging conceptual economy.

I asked myself these questions: Have corporations grown too big to be humane, understand customers, and react to the market quickly? What are the roles of enterprises in modern day socioeconomic environments? Is the relevance of the knowledge economy fading when it comes to preparing the modern day workforce? Is it time for us to revisit Drucker's mid-20th century take on entrepreneurship in America? These questions led me to find my way to Claremont in 1999 to take classes and work on a research paper with Peter Drucker himself.

Drucker has significantly influenced the way I think. I'm fascinated by the challenges that he imposed on his students to find the right solutions themselves following the right principles. He routinely emphasized and focused on the power of asking the right questions instead of telling people what to do. Though his principles can be misconstrued as a little vague, they have been proven to be the foundation. It's no wonder that presidents of sovereign nations, corporate CEOs, non-profit philanthropists, and religious evangelists have all borrowed his knowledge to accomplish amazing results.

As much as I admire Peter Drucker and borrow his wisdom whenever I can, as I've said, the knowledge economy that we are accustomed to is changing drastically at a rapid pace. To a certain extent, we mastered the craft of managing organizations, segregating the ones with knowledge (doctors, engineers, technologists, researchers, and MBAs) from those who lack formal education. The knowledge economy highly favored this segment of knowledge workers, who had a form of permanence in the corporate scenario. Jobs were secure to the point that knowledge workers didn't feel the need to be savvy in multidisciplinary skill sets.

In the second half of the 20th century, we also mastered the craft of measuring the success of corporations based on return on investors and shareholders.

In the conceptual economy, the general morale of the workforce is different, and founder dynamics are different.

The Rise of Incubators

"It is always the start that requires the greatest effort."
- James Cash Penney

I started the @4entrepreneur initiative in 2007 because I was frustrated that I couldn't find good resources for entrepreneurs, at least not collectively in one place. This site brought together thousands of entrepreneurs looking to both launch and scale. I was fascinated to get the kind of traffic that it received earlier in the launch. I always intended to keep it small and commercial-free, but the very first year we launched, some of our articles were featured as top stories on leading bookmarking sites. If I'm not mistaken, one of the articles on entrepreneurship posted on our blog is still ranked as one of the most visited articles. We went on to produce more than 20 entrepreneur television shows that aired on our blog and various networks.

What I learned while running that site are lessons I frequently use to this day. I interviewed many entrepreneurs, venture capitalists, celebrities turned entrepreneurs, political figures, and community leaders.

Some of my notable interviews included an exclusive with Rock 'n Roll Hall of Famer Bobby Womack. Rock legends rarely give interviews, so I was honored that Bobby consented. He passionately talked about his creative entrepreneurship journey and about following his passion throughout his life. I was shocked to recently learn that he has been diagnosed with the early stages of Alzheimer's disease. Telling stories of his struggles, his passionate pursuit of art, and making it as a creative entrepreneur, he couldn't help but inspire others to follow their own passions, either as creative artists or entrepreneurs.

In the years that followed, however, my focus shifted to running businesses in the private sector. Still, I always supported causes of entrepreneurship. I was particularly happy to see the emerging culture of mentorship via startup incubators.

Here are the three incubators that I am most fond of:

Y Combinator

I frequently covered articles on Y Combinator and the super startups that came out of there. Paul Graham founded Y Combinator, and as of this writing, Paul has brought in seven partners who have influential roles in investment communities. In terms of encouraging startups, Paul said, "The best way to find out if a product will work is to launch it." Y Combinator is considered one of the most influential incubators. Startups coming out of it receive enormous valuation for the right reasons.

The following introduction to the program is taken from the Y Combinator website verbatim: "In 2005, Y Combinator developed a new model of startup funding. Twice a year we invest a small amount of money ($14-20k + an $80k note) in a large number of startups (most recently 46). The startups move to Silicon Valley for 3 months, during which we work intensively with them to get the company into the best possible shape and refine their pitch to investors. Each cycle culminates in Demo Day, when the startups present to a large audience of investors. But YC doesn't end on Demo Day. We and the YC alumni network continue to help founders for the life of their company, and beyond."

This startup launch pad boasts a who's who in the world of investment and entrepreneurial leadership.

Mentors and investors at Y Combinator can play a vital role, connecting entrepreneurs with resources and deep networks. With diminishing barrier to entry, it is critical to have the right network of investors, mentors, and connectors like the ones that Y Combinator possesses.

Tech Stars

Boulder, Colorado-based Tech Stars has emerged as another powerful network to launch startups. Unlike Y Combinator, Tech Stars conducts events across the United States and offers great platforms for entrepreneurs coming from places other than the Silicon Valley. As of this writing, about 40 percent of the startups come from areas near the city of each program.

David Cohen founded Tech Stars, and he says, "The entire community has started to see high quality accelerators as a filtering mechanism. It's become a new college for entrepreneurs because we are so selective on the front end." Tech Stars is a 13-week program that was launched in conjunction with President Obama's Startup America Partnership.

SendGrid was one of Tech Stars' innovative 2009 graduates. According to the company website, "SendGrid's cloud-based email infrastructure relieves businesses of the cost and complexity of maintaining custom email systems. SendGrid provides reliable delivery, scalability and real-time analytics along with flexible APIs that make custom integration a breeze."

The company has raised more than $27 million in venture capital funds.

At this moment, Tech Stars comprises 150 active companies with average funding for each company at $1.5 million at an 80.65 percent success rate, and ten percent of the companies have been acquired.

500 Startups

One of my personal favorites is 500 Startups. It's based in Silicon Valley but attracts startups from around the world. Investment funds from around the country go to 500 Startups to find investment opportunities. According to its CrunchBase profile, "500 Startups is an early-stage seed fund and incubator program located in Mountain View, CA." They invest primarily in consumer and SMB Internet startups, as well as related web infrastructure services. Their initial investment size is typically $25,000-$250,000. Selected areas of interest include financial services and e-commerce, search/social/mobile platforms, personal and business productivity, education and language, family and healthcare, and web infrastructure.

I know that regional investment funds like Vegas Tech Fund travel to 500 Startups' Demo Days to find companies in which to invest. I personally like the event, as it invites applicants from New Delhi to startups based out of London, England.

500 Startups is a great example of conceptual thinking. I have strongly believed all along that innovative startups can emerge from any part of the world in the same fashion that investors can represent any part of the world. Geographic restrictions are no longer a deciding factor when it comes to investing in companies in the conceptual economy.

Your Local Coffee Shop
is Your New Corner Office

The Freemont Street Experience represents the rich history of Las Vegas dating back to 1905 when Vegas was founded. It's the second most famous street in the city. To this day, Freemont Street possesses that sense of "old Las Vegas," where you find the crowd reminiscing about their experiences in their teen years.

During summer days, the street hosts free concert series and BBQ contests. Between three large concert stages, the legends of rock 'n roll like Guns N' Roses,

Poison, and Survivor share the same stages with local rock artists. You will find super talented street artists who create artwork on the spot, as they try to sell it to amazed tourists. You will see impersonators of Elvis, Al Pacino, and Marilyn Monroe working the crowd, getting their pictures taken with tourists for a couple of bucks. People from all over the world visit the street.

Freemont has modernized its hotels, malls, and restaurants without losing that sense of old vibe Las Vegas. Historically, the western end of Freemont Street was featured in many classic films and television shows from the James Bond flick, "Diamonds are Forever," to the 2007 Nicolas Cage film, "Next," where Cage is featured in the Golden Nugget from the Freemont Street Experience. As a lover of art and cinema, I admire the history of Vegas and old Hollywood.

But as I've said, times have changed. Blended among the tourists, middle-aged rock 'n roll fanatics, and, of course, Vegas underground artists, you will find the new breed of college educated transplants to the city from different parts of the world. And this is great for the city, as this new group of transplants is incentivized to start companies and create jobs in Vegas.

Until as recently as a couple of years ago, tourists and local urbanites avoided this part of town. Today, hip restaurants, bars, and nightclubs are popping up. With strong incentives from the city, companies small and large are starting to flock into this part of town. It has, in a way, built its own mini-culture and ecosystem for local entrepreneurs from all walks of life.

Regardless of which vertical you are in, if you're interested in pursuing an entrepreneurial career or simply want to participate in the economic boom about to happen in DTP (what locals call the Downtown Project), you will find leaders and contributors at Beat Coffee House and Records. From the outside, it's an unassuming coffee shop on the Eastern side of Freemont Street. But if you walk inside the Beat, you will find art galleries, a tech incubator, co-working space, and a series of service-oriented companies ranging from advertising agencies and web developers to social media consultants. The Beat is the center of the Las Vegas entrepreneurial ecosystem.

Coffee shops like the Beat are the new corner offices for entrepreneurs. Places like these are where big deals, networking, and socializing on a Monday afternoon take place. Each town has its own Beat coffeehouse.

As a conceptual entrepreneur, it isn't enough just to be savvy online or network with your Facebook, Twitter, or LinkedIn buddies. You have to get out there and see what's going on in your neighborhood and community.

As a local community leader or just somebody who cares about where you live and raise your family, you need to have more of a vested interest in your community than international corporations or investors getting in the game for the wrong reasons.

I encourage entrepreneurs to get involved with passion and meaning within their communities. Do something for the greater good. I'm positive that as a result, you will be more successful in your entrepreneurial career.

For entrepreneurs, with modern technologies and the new, amazing unbiased ecosystems of inter-entrepreneurial clusters, the notion of making it locally and thinking globally with a conceptual mind has never been more relevant.

The Role of Public-Private Partnerships at the Local Level

"A genuine leader is not a searcher for consensus but a molder of consensus."
- Martin Luther King, Jr.

As I have mentioned, I'm proud to be associated with the meaningful non-profit initiative, Startup America Partnership, as a region champion for the state of Nevada. Under the leadership of President Obama, this initiative is a tremendous resource for entrepreneurs, especially those in parts of the U.S. that don't receive the attention of entrepreneurial hubs like Silicon Valley and New York City.

In Nevada, we have launched the following initiatives:

Explore Nano
Explore Biomed
Eco Entrepreneur Initiative

We have also supported Project Vesto, Startup Weekend, and the Downtown Speaker Series. Additionally, we have collaborated with the existing @4entrepreneur initiative, which has spent more than seven years fostering entrepreneurship.

Having lived in five different states during the last 20 years (New York, California, Nevada, Kansas, and Michigan), I share the sentiments of Startup America's mission statement as presented in Ewing Marion Kauffman's Foundation report, *The Startup Rising Eighteen Months of the Startup America Partnership*: "Too many entrepreneurs are disconnected from each other; from their communities; from their towns, cities, and states; from potential customers, funders, and talent; and the guiding principles for this operating system are: a belief in loose communities of entrepreneurs rather than an organizational hierarchy; propagating from what exists, rather than creating from scratch; embracing, not resisting, disruption; patience to develop communities over years, not weeks; celebrating success; and, above all, focusing on entrepreneurs."

National leader Donna Harris, who was instrumental in the success of Startup America Partnership, believed in letting the regions flourish on their own rather than controlled by headquarters. I have started and scaled companies in three different states, so I firmly agree that regions hold unique personalities and cultures.

Trying to apply one strategy that worked in one region to another region is not practical and is doomed.

Startup regions have used different strategies to foster their local regions. Startup Nevada has played cheerleader for Startup Weekend Elko (a small rural Nevada town in between Reno and Salt Lake City) and Startup Weekend Las Vegas. Daniel Herr, another startup champion based in Reno, has been an instrumental quiet crusader supporting local entrepreneurial hubs in Northern Nevada. Through NIREC-sponsored Project Vesto, Startup America supported it fully from Day 1 and has played a vital role in connecting entrepreneurs between Southern and Northern Nevada.

Andy White, another region champion, has been very supportive in connecting the Vegas Tech community, Vegas Tech Fund, and Downtown Project with Startup Nevada.

At the forefront of the culture of return on community, Nevada's startup clusters and redevelopment projects have helped revitalize communities, and more private investors in Nevada are focusing on projects that benefit the community. Startup Nevada has leveraged the existing list of entrepreneurial events and works organized by multiple entities from NIREC, Lake Tahoe Fund, Downtown Project, and many smaller Startup Nevada meetups that have brought together bonds between entrepreneurs throughout the state.

We are a dedicated bunch that believes in getting stuff done and not waiting for leadership to dictate. My initial statewide strategy was to plug into what worked and not to reinvent the wheel. Following this strategy, we are complementing the great work of the Downtown Project, as well as the work of the Vegas Tech community.

With a strong band of entrepreneurs, the Vegas Tech community is committed to assembling a team of Las Vegas-based entrepreneurs and businesses to collectively represent at this year's SXSW. We strongly believe in supporting them in this endeavor.

Startup Nevada is working closely with a new Las Vegas International Film Festival as well to find ways to foster creative entrepreneurship by supporting theater and cinema.

What Social Media Means
for Entrepreneurs

"We now accept the fact that learning is a lifelong process of keeping abreast of change. And the most pressing task is to teach people how to learn."
- Peter Drucker

I recently read a random humorous tweet from someone I can't recall. They said that in London there are more social media consultants than kids. I can understand the light take on so-called social media experts. I recall similar hype when dotcom and e-commerce consultants ruled "back in the day." People didn't understand the depth of the new medium, and business models were created without proper foresight and sustainable planning.

You have probably heard of cases like eVan, which painted its fleet the same week it went bankrupt, or another e-commerce company called eToys that signed a ten-year lease for its Santa Monica headquarters just to fold the same year. People running these enterprises were bright entrepreneurs and executives, but they obviously received bad advice from consultants, advisors, or even venture capitalists and investors.

Are we seeing history repeat itself in the social media space? Only time will tell. An analogy can certainly be drawn between the many social media-based companies out there today and the e-commerce businesses of the not too distant past. But we sense that it's different this time around. First of all, the Internet has matured. E-commerce has seen major success stories, including the survivors of the dotcom era like Amazon and eBay.

Social media by itself is just a medium if you look at it objectively. An interesting aspect of social media is that it has become an amazing enabler for everybody to carry their messages to their circle of influence. The need to come up with fundamentally sound, sustainable products and services has not changed.

Just like in the heyday of the Internet and e-commerce, when the dust settles, there will only be a few truly sustainable companies that will deliver the medium itself. The rest will be the beneficiaries of the medium to create various unique business models in their own respective verticals.

One area of social media that fascinates me is the vast data/information that is readily available within it. Data without proper structure and purpose is useless, however. This new many-to-many medium is creating an endless supply of random data, and this fact calls for conceptual entrepreneurs to come up with innovative ideas to make use of it all. This data can be used in a vast number of arenas from healthcare to public awareness.

The Role of Entrepreneurs
in the New "New Deal"

"The only thing we know about the future is that it will be different."
- Peter Drucker

In the time of the Great Depression, visionary U.S. President Franklin D. Roosevelt laid out a series of bold initiatives under the plan famously known as the "New Deal."

The New Deal was created mainly to stimulate the economy, come up with short-term aid for the unemployed, and provide much needed reform of the economic and banking systems. FDR's bold outlook provided a strong foundation for growth and brought a new direction for a country entangled in laissez-faire governance. FDR's New Deal was instrumental in bringing economic recovery during most of the latter part of the 20th century. Some of the measures taken under the New Deal (FDIC, SEC, Social Security) in the 1930s continue to have a strong impact on the country to this day. This strong post-Depression era governance, along with the consistent economic upturn, provided a healthy breeding ground for the rising entrepreneurial culture in America.

Historians have compared the FDR administration with the Obama administration, as both presidents came to the office needing to take drastic measures to stabilize the economy and bring about changes that would have a long-term impact on the economy.

I think the analogy ends there, however. There is a stark contrast between the strategy that FDR had to take and what the nation is going through right now. These are rapidly changing times. The conceptual economy demands change and an emphasis once again on what made this country great. We need to take a serious look at the entrepreneurial foundation that the forefathers built. If history is a guide, strong governance will help, but entrepreneurship flourished on its own in the 20th century. In the conceptual economy, good governance alone will not be enough to keep entrepreneurs competitive when rapidly growing economies around the world are catching up fast.

I was encouraged after meeting President Obama during his recent visit to Las Vegas. It was an honor and a pleasure to be invited by the White House to attend his policy speech. So many entrepreneurs are looking to the President to guide them on some of the pending policies related to entrepreneurship. The Crowdfunding bill, for example, as a part of the Jobs Act, is in its final stages. This bill offers tremendous opportunities and resources for aspiring entrepreneurs, enabling entrepreneurs to avoid a lot of red tape and reach out for resources and capital in order to execute their ideas.

In the conceptual economy, it should be the utmost priority for everybody to consciously talk about fostering entrepreneurship, which means directly and indirectly providing a sustainable plan to strengthen the economy.

Since I first wrote an article in this field on my blog some four years ago, I am pleased to share some of the progress. I had written extensively about the immediate need to have public-private partnerships like Startup America and to reach out to the areas often ignored by the entrepreneurial ecosystems. This program is a great resource center for aspiring entrepreneurs looking to take the plunge.

With help of organizations like Startup America, folks in the heartland and other small towns across the United States are getting a lot of attention. But this is just a start. The reason Silicon Valley is Silicon Valley today is because of the amazing talent, investors, and resources that it attracts to the region. In order for an ecosystem to flourish, the region needs the perfect combination of ideas, talent, angels, venture capitalists, and mentors. It is not possible for everybody to be everywhere. This is why connectors like the Startup America Partnership can play a key role in facilitating much-needed collaborations.

Steve Case and his Revolution Fund is a great example of a venture fund that takes chances on ventures outside of Silicon Valley. It is my understanding that Case intends to invest 80 percent of his funds in startups coming out of other places. He is especially interested in investing heavily in startups out of the Midwest states that are often ignored by the mainstream venture capital community.

One of the parent organizations that's playing a supporting role is The Kauffman Foundation, a non-profit dedicated to fostering entrepreneurship. It backs many entrepreneurial initiatives, including the Startup America Partnership. Organizations like Kauffman have emerged as leaders in fostering a society of economically independent individuals who are engaged citizens, contributing to the improvement of their communities.

Creative Entrepreneurship and Hollywood

"Doing the right thing is more important than doing the thing right."
- Peter Drucker

Just like in other verticals, the entertainment space will also be drastically affected by the new economy. I dabbled in the conceptual development of television and films early on and had a chance to work with some prominent names in the entertainment industry, including Academy Award-nominated director Arthur Hiller, Academy Award-nominated screenwriter Douglas Day

Stewart, and multiple Emmy Award-winning CBS anchor Mario Machado. I learned a great deal from these exceptionally creative souls.

While living in Los Angeles, I came across many creative types who often struggle to balance mastering their craft with marketing themselves. Creative professions, by nature, are highly competitive when it comes to monetary gains. Creative types disregard the realistic aspect of making it and truly follow their passion. And, by all means, they should give their best to mastering their craft, but being a little bit entrepreneurial would also make a lot of sense.

The fundamentals of entrepreneurship apply in the creative domain as well as other arenas. Highly successful entertainers are savvy entrepreneurs. Mick Jagger, though hard to believe, attended the prestigious

London School of Economics and has strong entrepreneurial acumen; Oprah Winfrey has built her media empire and has now started her own network, keeping entrepreneurial spirit alive all along the way.

Think outside the box! It's okay to focus on non-glamorous ventures while honing your craft. A notable screenwriter friend of mine built a post-production business that transcribed for studios and production companies after he finished his internship at a major studio. He was extremely passionate about building this venture. He became so successful that after building a solid clientele and track record, he sold the company. With his newfound fortune, he was able to focus full-time on screenwriting. He successfully sold his first screenplay the following year for half a million dollars in a bidding war between multiple studios. The takeaway is that his dynamic personality, along with his passion for both business and his craft, allowed him to be successful in both areas. So, the lesson is that creative types *must* learn to be entrepreneurs.

Leverage social media. Social media is a great on-ramp tool to connect with influencers, executives, studios, and production companies. There is a plethora of applications being created, making social media the tool to connect with end users. A company I'm involved with uses mobile devices to interact with live television events. Our technology enables major advertisers to interact with customers and fans via Twitter, eliminating the expense of traditional media like radio and television.

How can a solo creative entrepreneur build a presence on Twitter and Facebook to connect with the entertainment industry?
Be exceptional at what you do!

This may sound like simple advice, but, in reality, this is the foundation for everything that follows. You can have ICM and CAA represent you, but at the end of the day, if you aren't exceptional at what you do, you probably won't make it. In a creative field, just like in any other field, there is a large portion that has to do with God-given, innate talent. The rest has to do with dedicating everything you have to mastering your passion. Once you have your craft mastered, then you want to push your presence on social, as well as, traditional media networks.

Trust is everything! To be an influencer or get noticed in social media, winning trust is essential. Impacting within social media is not a popularity contest. It's better to have a small pool of like-minded people in your vertical group than a random large following.

Once you have your social network in place, the beauty of social media tools like Twitter is that followers are already opted in, so you can communicate with them directly (direct messaging) without coming across as a spammer. Even with the ones who are not following you, you can interact by addressing them directly and publicly via a tweet.

Social media is *just* a medium. Social media tools like blogs, Twitter, Facebook, MySpace, and Four Square are just tools. Smart, creative entrepreneurs must learn to use them appropriately and not as a fad.

Once you choose the right social media tool, the message still has to be effective. Higher frequency of messages does not translate to higher effectiveness. Articulate your message, keep your value proposition simple, and follow the priceless advice from the world of sales: KISS – Keep It Simple Stupid!

Think like an investor investing in your own creative venture. Treat your passion as an entrepreneurial venture or career. Before spending anytime on social media, think of it like a venture. Proceed as if you were paying someone else to do it. What would you ask them to do?

Bottom line: Make sure the time is being spent wisely, and you are not distracted from the craft that you should be mastering instead. Creative entrepreneurship is truly an *art* of business.

Always add value! The creative arena can be self-centered and narcissistic at times, so it's easier to forget to help others succeed before focusing on yourself. The reality is that if you help your fellow artists succeed, you are creating a roadmap for your own success! It isn't a coincidence that most major producers, directors, screenwriters, and artists supported each other prior to becoming famous. Most likely, they parted ways when they made it big, but just like mega-business moguls, most of the entertainment moguls had that supporting camaraderie early on in their careers.

I would love to hear from creative entrepreneurs out there! Feel free to shoot me an email at ideas4entrepreneurs@gmail.com.

Picasso once said, "Every child is an artist. The problem is how to remain an artist once we grow up." Creativity, entrepreneurial spirit, and innovative drive can die when we grow older. Life happens, and priorities shift. But for the select group of creative entrepreneurs, the passion lives on, and they make sure they turn their respective crafts into meaningful, fulfilling careers.

The more I interact with entertainers from all ages and demographics, I find one common concern: how to sustain a career in these highly competitive fields. In my first meeting with the 80-year-old director, Arthur Hiller, at his Beverly Hills office back in 2001, he shared the secret behind the longevity of his career. Hiller was different in his peer group. He had a Masters degree in Psychology and always stayed grounded, truly following his passion and focusing on filmmaking. He successfully went on to direct 33 major studio releases, including several classics.

Besides Hiller, I have worked with many notable professional athletes and entertainers, and I can firmly say that the sentiment among all has been the same. It's extremely important *to treat your craft as a sustainable creative entrepreneurial venture.*

A creative career and sustaining business competitiveness are more similar than I had previously thought. The age old mantra to succeed in business is the same as maintaining a competitive advantage. I see smart people day in and day out with the highest level of intellect crashing and burning in spite of their great ideas and initial multimillion dollar funding. This happens on every scale from mom and pop stores around the corner to major Fortune 500 companies. If you fail to know your customers, adapt quickly, sustain your competitiveness, and *add value,* you will crash.

The key is to be able to understand your customers early on and do everything that your resources allow to master your craft and add that all-important value.

The analogy for the entertainment industry is the same. You have to understand your fans if you are a studio, a screenwriter, the record industry, a musician, etc.

Unbiased Connectivity:
A Global Perspective

"If your actions inspire others to dream more, learn more, do more and become more, you are a leader."
- John Quincy Adams

Cloud Factory is a venture-backed company founded and led by veteran entrepreneur Mark Sears. It has an amazing mission and is committed to creating more than one million jobs in developing nations.

Mark and his talented team moved their entire families to Kathmandu, Nepal. The company is very inspirational to the whole entrepreneurial community and especially to the young, educated, and talented workforce based in Kathmandu like Akar Anil, who is an avid social media user who works at Cloud Factory.

Cloud Factory has been instrumental in giving back to the local community. It recently led an initiative to sponsor the first Startup Weekend event in Kathmandu. Going through the live Twitter feeds from SWK was very inspiring, and as a result, I couldn't help but reflect on the tremendous changes that are taking place around the globe.

Cloud Factory is unique in the sense that it's trying to change the way outsourcing is done. They have a unique cloud-based business model, capable of scaling at a level unheard of before, and this scale and reliability is very attractive to American companies that outsource their jobs.

In the past, non-enterprise-level projects were outsourced on an individual, small scale basis. As a result, quality while trying to scale was often compromised. Cloud Factory intends to scale in a way that it will create a platform in ruby on rails (the new scale platform to build apps based on technology infrastructure) for talent from beyond Nepal to join forces and reach that million employee mark. Already, this Kathmandu-based company is sending (or inviting to be on the Cloud Factory platform) work to India and other parts of the world.

What companies and conceptual entrepreneurs in the western world need to know is that scaling resources for your next company can come from the least expected regions of the world.

I have had an opportunity to travel around the world and cities within the U.S. many times over, and I've seen the state of entrepreneurship firsthand. While in London, it was great to be able to connect with students, entrepreneurs, and faculty at the London School of Business and the London School of Economics. I found the entrepreneurial spirit to be high among students, but not as high as I found in the Silicon Valley and other parts of the United States. However, entrepreneurial spirit is very high among non-elite university students outside of the confines of college campuses. I have also found that entrepreneurs from England collaborate well with entrepreneurs here in the United States.

Entrepreneurial hubs like 500 Startups, SXSW, and the Startup America Partnership regularly feature companies from across the pond. In the past, the UK government got involved and showed efforts to foster entrepreneurship by funding directly in venture funds. The results and effects are as yet unclear, however.

I don't often like to focus on the macro aspect of the global economy and instead focus on results-oriented local stories from the trenches, but here is my quick, positive take on the EU entrepreneurship scene. Even though entrepreneurial success stories in the EU are not as common as you would find in the United States, I found London as a business hub to be quite impressive. I'm sure the entrepreneurial ecosystem there will continually play a critical role in the conceptual economy.

Due to its great geographic location, London is home to over 500 international banking and financial institutes, which is more than New York City and Los Angeles combined. The EU also has that ease of mobility for entrepreneurs within member nations that can potentially give quite a sustainable competitive edge for the whole region.

With leading innovation hubs and the long presence of remarkable higher institutions, the world will continue to see innovative enterprises like Nokia and IKEA emerging from small EU nations.

Our Entrepreneurial Initiative

More than 30 entrepreneurs/alumni from London Business School, London School of Economics, the University of Southern California, the University of Nevada Las Vegas, the University of Nevada Reno, Indian Institute of Technology, and veteran NASA, JPL alums have teamed up to explore opportunities in emerging technologies like mobile technologies and social media. Our goal is to create an ecosystem from which innovation will emerge from the transatlantic collaboration and active participation of entrepreneurs around the world.

Next Stop...Mumbai, India

My visit with many Indian entrepreneurs reminded me of Khanna's book, "Billions of Entrepreneurs: How China and India Are Reshaping Their Futures–and Yours." The difference that I found between this trip and my last trip to India four years back is that the raw entrepreneurial spirit there as a whole has shifted to a structured approach to entrepreneurship. I was not surprised to see that one of the finalists this year at the Silicon Valley-based 500 Startups came from India.

Entrepreneurs are more readily realizing the need for sustainability and a structured approach to starting up companies. Even more interesting, they are also realizing the need for larger awareness and the importance of creating a properly trained workforce. The closest analogy that I can think of is the emergence of the knowledge economy in the early 1950s in the United States when corporate America struggled to get its workforce ready. The movement officially labeled during that time was "industrial discipline." India and other parts of the Indian subcontinent are seeing a movement comparable to that era of industrial discipline, and that is great news for the entrepreneurs of the world.

What are the Opportunities for Western-Trained Conceptual Entrepreneurs?

What the booming Asian economy currently needs is a flock of western-trained infrastructure consultants. With 60 percent of college graduates focusing on engineering and medical fields, countries like India and China do not lack innovation. In the case of India, with the population exceeding the billion mark, the nation doesn't lack a workforce for menial labor either. What India lacks are high level executives for medium-sized companies. India has its share of smart management consultants— McKinsey types for large enterprises. But the majority of mid-size organizations (20-500 employees) are seriously lacking higher caliber management, and these companies are open-minded and seeking help!

The real opportunity for conceptual entrepreneurs is that the consuming capacity of nations like China and

India is quite staggering. India is certainly more than the place where call center calls are answered. The rate that infrastructure and housing development is taking place is noteworthy. Just like any rapid economic growth, this raw exponential growth brings about enormous opportunities for the savvy group of U.S.-based conceptual entrepreneurs.

While the upwardly mobile Indian community, by culture, tends to focus on higher brands and firms with name recognition, there is an opportunity for smaller firms and solo U.S.-based entrepreneurs to think strategically and capture the market from the bottom up.

Future Entrepreneurs

"Do not go where the path may lead, go instead where there is no path and leave a trail."
- Ralph Waldo Emerson

During my recent visit to Nepal, I had the chance to be a guest speaker for MBA students at two innovative colleges in Kathmandu, something I had wanted to do for a long time. Even though it was a short encounter, it was a great homecoming for me, as I had received my own earlier education at St. Xavier's Catholic School.

Speaking to a highly motivated group of students at the ACE Institute of Management and the Kathmandu University School of Management had me thinking how small the world has become. This has truly become an era when ideas can emerge from any corner of the world. Barrier to entry has come down so sharply that students are taking on amazing feats.

An MIT graduate recently returned to Kathmandu to collaborate with a major bank to introduce mobile cash—the idea floating around in Silicon Valley for a while that actually got implemented successfully here.

The concept makes more sense and finds more practical use in Nepal with over 15 million smart phone subscribers (3.2 million subscribers joining just within this last year in a total population of just over 30 million).

Being a successful entrepreneur is not about following glamour but is about being able to find pain points in the areas where nobody else is looking. It's also about being savvy enough to fill the void in the most pragmatic and economical way.

There is also always that emotional aspect of being an entrepreneur, of doing the right thing and trying to make a difference while you're at it. Exploring ideas with the students at ACE and KU that can make people's lives better are the types of projects that keep me motivated to be an entrepreneur.